THE CREED

A Worship Anthology on

THE CREED

H.J.Richards

Kevin
Mayhew

First published in 1996 by
KEVIN MAYHEW LTD
Rattlesden
Bury St Edmunds
Suffolk IP30 0SZ

ISBN 0 86209 727 4
Catalogue No 1500036

Front cover:
Regina Sanctorum. Anonymous, Aesthetic Movement, c. 1900.
Courtesy of Cooper Fine Art. Reproduced by kind permission
of Fine Art Photographic Library, London.

Cover design by Graham Johnstone and Veronica Ward
Typesetting and Page Creation by Louise Hill
Printed and bound in Great Britain.

CONTENTS

FOREWORD

The warm reception given to the two worship anthologies I have recently published (one for Christmas and one for Easter) has encouraged me to forage even further afield to collect a greater variety of biblical texts, poems, readings, meditations and prayers which could be used for worship at other times of the year.

In this volume I have grouped the anthology around the Christian Creed, which was first formulated in the second century as the profession of faith to be made by candidates for baptism. Its clear trinitarian framework (God, Christ, Holy Spirit) has been copied by all creeds written since, and conveniently provides the main chapter headings under which I have placed the excerpts I have chosen. That these should be followed by chapters on Faith and Praise will be welcomed by those who recognise the Trinity not as a theological problem, but as an invitation to praise God.

H. J. RICHARDS

1 THE CREED

I believe in God the Father Almighty,
maker of heaven and earth:

And in Jesus Christ his only Son our Lord,
who was conceived by the Holy Ghost,
born of the Virgin Mary,
suffered under Pontius Pilate,
was crucified, dead, and buried,
he descended into hell;
the third day he rose again from the dead,
he ascended into heaven,
and sitteth on the right hand of God the Father Almighty;
from thence he shall come to judge the quick and the dead.

I believe in the Holy Ghost;
the holy Catholic Church;
the Communion of Saints;
the Forgiveness of Sins;
the Resurrection of the body;
and the life everlasting. Amen.

BOOK OF COMMON PRAYER.

Christians believe in the God whom Jesus called *Father* who gives life
to all things.

Christians believe in the man from Nazareth
who brought that mysterious God close to us,
who showed what it means to be a *Son of God,*
who was willing to die for his belief,
who lives on, by the power of God, in his friends,
who will come again to say who his real friends are.

Christians believe in the friends of Jesus,
who live the way he did, in his *Spirit,*
who bring God close to all other people,
who tell people the good news that they are forgiven,
who build up peace on earth,
who know that a better world is possible,
and who work to make it come true.

TRS. H. J. RICHARDS (B.1921)

I believe in the God, to whom,
in the Spirit of Jesus, we may say,
Abba Father;
the creative source
and the future.

And in Jesus,
God's Servant and well-beloved Son,
who came to us completely from God,
and in whom God's whole fullness
dwells bodily;
who worked for our healing,
who transcended human limitations,
and spoke words of eternal life;
who for that reason was rejected,
but suffered for the sake of our liberation,
and died on the cross;
who was raised from death by God
to live in us,
and to be the centre and future of all creation.

I believe in the Spirit of God and of Jesus,
who speaks through prophets,
and leads us to the full truth.
I confess God's Kingdom,
now and in eternity,
and the Church which longs for and serves this Kingdom.
I confess the liberation from sins,
and the power to love,
and the new creation
in which justice dwells,
where God will be all in all.
Amen.

TRS. PIET SCHOONENBERG

I believe in the living God,
father of Jesus Christ our Lord,
our God, our almighty father.

He has created the world, all things
in his only beloved son,
the image and likeness of his glory.

Jesus, light of eternal light,
word of God, faithful, abiding,
Jesus Christ, our grace and our truth.

In order to serve this world of ours,
in order to share our human lot,
he became flesh of our human flesh.

By the will of the Holy Spirit,
and born of the virgin Mary,
he became man, a man like us.

He was broken for our sins
and was obedient unto death
and gave himself upon the cross.

Therefore he has received the name
of the firstborn from the dead,
the son of God and Lord of all.

He will come in God's own time
to do justice to the living and the dead.
He is the man whom I shall resemble.

I believe in the power of the Spirit,
in the love of the father and the son,
in the covenant of God with men,

in the Church, the body of Christ,
called together and sent forth
to do the work that he has done –

to enlighten and to serve,
and to bear the sins of the world,
and to build up peace on earth.

I believe that we shall arise from death
with a new, undying body,
for he is the God of the living.

Amen. Come, Lord Jesus, come.

TRS. HUUB OOSTERHUIS

I believe in God, Creator and Sustainer of all life,
deepest Silence and brightest Truth,
who made us to be in relationship
with each other and with God.

I believe in Jesus, Healer of hurts,
Enabler of the powerless,
who named us as his friends
and called us as disciples in the Way of the Kingdom,
who died at the hands of those
who found truth too painful
and who rose in the power of love.

I believe in the Spirit of Wisdom, Truth and Love,
who calls us to be our whole selves,
who challenges us to stand up for justice,
to be makers of peace
and builders of the Kingdom.

I believe in the true life
which springs ever fresh, green, vital, abundant,
playful and full of joy,
and which chases out darkness and dryness and death.

ANNE LEWIS

2 GOD HIDDEN

Scripture Readings

There is a time for everything
that is under the sun.

A time to plant, and a time to reap,
a time to give, and a time to keep:
is this the meaning of life, my friend?
Where does it get you in the end?

A time for war, and a time for peace,
a time for kissing, and a time to cease:
is this the meaning of life, my friend?
Where does it get you in the end?

A time to lose, and a time to seek,
a time for silence, and a time to speak:
is this the meaning of life, my friend?
Where does it get you in the end?

A time to laugh, and a time to cry,
a time for birth, and a time to die:
is this the meaning of life, my friend?
Lord, O Lord, send whom you will send.

BOOK OF ECCLESIASTES 3:1-8

Our ears hear
our fathers tell us the story
of what you did for them
    in times past
You gave victories to Israel
    because we did not trust in our weapons
    and tanks did not give us the victory

But now you have abandoned us
you have strengthened their systems of government
you have upheld their regimes and their Party
We are displaced persons
refugees without passports
prisoners of concentration camps
condemned to forced labour
condemned to the gas chamber
consumed in the crematoria
    and our ashes are scattered
We are the people of Auschwitz
    of Buchenwald of Belsen of Dachau

With our skin they made lampshades
and with our fat they made soap
As sheep to the slaughter
you let them haul us off to the gas chambers . . .
we went in naked
    and there they locked shut the doors and extinguished all lights
    and you covered us with the shadows of death
Nothing survived of us but mountains of clothes
mountains of toys
    and mountains of shoes . . .

And now you are a hidden God
Why do you hide your face
forgetful of our suffering and of our oppression?
Arise
    and help us!
For your own honour!

PSALM 44 (43)
TRS. ERNESTO CARDENAL (B. 1915)

Why God Hides Himself

We talk about creation as revealing God, and natural theology is built upon that proposition. But you could equally well argue that the purpose of creation is to hide God, because we could not withstand the intolerable impact of total reality. Demosthenes said, 'If you cannot bear the candle, how will you face the sun?' And we can't bear the candle. We live within the finest of tolerances. If our temperatures rise or fall by a handful of degrees, we're dead. Too much pressure, too little pressure, and we implode or we explode. Too much noise, too much silence, and we go mad. We live within the finest of tolerances, we can bear only a tiny fragment of reality. How could we bear the total impact of the reality of God? Which is why God said to Moses, 'No man can look upon my face and live.'

There's a West African creation myth that puts this point I think very neatly. In the beginning God was naked God. And people were afraid to go near him. So God clothed himself with the mantle of creation. He wrapped himself in forests where people could hunt, and in rivers where they could fish, and in soil that they could cultivate. And so, says the myth, men lost their fear of God, and God was as happy as a dog with fleas.

COLIN MORRIS

The Night is Dark

Lead, kindly light, amid th'encircling gloom,
    lead thou me on;
the night is dark and I am far from home,
    lead thou me on.
Keep thou my feet; I do not ask to see
    the distant scene; one step enough for me.

I was not ever thus, nor prayed that thou
    shouldst lead me on;
I loved to choose and see my path; but now
    lead thou me on.
I loved the garish day, and, spite of fears,
    pride ruled my will; remember not past years.

So long thy power hath blest me, sure it still
    will lead me on
o'er moor and fen, o'er crag and torrent, till
    the night is gone;
and with the morn those angel faces smile
    which I have loved long since, and lost awhile.

JOHN HENRY NEWMAN (1801-1890)

Silent God

I believe in the sun
    even when it's not shining.
I believe in love
    even when I don't feel it.
I believe in God,
    even when he is silent.

JEWISH INSCRIPTION ON A CELLAR WALL IN WAR-TIME COLOGNE.

The Unknown God

I passed along the water's edge,
below the humid trees,
my spirit rocked in evening light,
the rushes round my knees,
my spirit rocked in sleep and sighs,
and saw the moorfowl pace
all dripping on a grassy slope,
and saw them cease to chase
each other round in circles,
and heard the eldest speak:

'Who holds the world between His bill,
and made us strong or weak,
is an undying moorfowl,
and He lives beyond the sky;
the rains are from His dripping wing,
the moonbeams from His eye.'

I passed a little further on,
and heard a lotus talk:
'Who made the world and ruleth it,
He hangeth on a stalk;
for I am in His image made
and all His tinkling tide
is but a sliding drop of rain
between His petals wide.'

A little way within the gloom,
a roebuck raised his eyes,
brimful of starlight, and he said:
'The Stamper of the skies,
He is a gentle Roebuck,
for how else, I pray, could He
conceive a thing so sad and soft,
a gentle thing like me?'

I passed a little further on
and heard a Peacock say:
'Who made the grass, and made the worms,
and made my feathers gay?
He is a monstrous Peacock,
and he waveth all the night
His languid tail above us,
lit with myriad spots of light.'

W. B. YEATS (1865-1939)

God Behind All

When a child in his play breaks something valuable, his mother does not love the breakage. But if later on her son goes far away or dies, she thinks of the incident with infinite tenderness, because she now sees it only as one of the signs of her child's existence. It is in this way that we ought to love God through everything good and everything evil, without distinction. If we love only through what is good, then it is not God we are loving but something earthly to which we give that name. We must not try to reduce evil to good by seeking compensations or justifications for evil. We must love God through the evil that occurs, solely because everything that actually occurs is real, and behind all reality stands God.

SIMONE WEIL (1909-1943)

Darkness

We tend to fret over our darkness, as if it were our own fault.
We cry out for enlightenment:

> Lighten our darkness, we beseech thee, O Lord
> Lead kindly light, amid the encircling gloom
> Send forth your light and your truth, let these be my guide

as if we couldn't live unless we knew all the answers. But we can.
Indeed we must. Even as he was writing *Lead kindly light*,
Newman knew that:

> I do not ask to see the distant scene:
> One step enough for me.

As Rabbi Eliezer Berkovits put it:

> If there is no answer,
> it is better to live without it
> than to find peace
> either in the sham of an insensitive faith
> or in the humbug of a belief that has eaten its fill.

Huub Oosterhuis puts it even more paradoxically in these words:

> Again and again, prayer is not knowing who God is,
> calling him by weak and questionable names.
> But he is not our names, our words.
> He is not as we think he is . . .
> Is God the light – is he the broad light of day?
> No, he is darkness, deep night, the void.
> He is not a lofty tree, but a shapeless twig,
> not the vast sea, but a glass of water,
> not a powerful voice, but a vulnerable silence . . .

H. J. RICHARDS (B.1921)

A Presence

I have learned
to look on nature, not as in the hour
of thoughtless youth; but hearing often-times
the still, sad music of humanity,
nor harsh nor grating, though of ample power
to chasten and subdue. And I have felt
a presence that disturbs me with the joy
of elevated thoughts, a sense sublime
of something far more deeply interfused,
whose dwelling is the light of setting suns,
and the round ocean and the living air,
and the blue sky, and in the mind of man:
a motion and a spirit that impels
all thinking things, all objects of all thought,
and rolls through all things.

WILLIAM WORDSWORTH (1770-1850)

A Great Cry

Blowing through heaven and earth,
and in our hearts and the heart of every living thing,
is a gigantic breath – a great Cry – which we call God.
Plant life wishes to continue
its motionless sleep next to stagnant waters,
but the Cry leaped up within it
and violently shook its roots:
'Away, let go of the earth, walk!'
Had the tree been able to think and judge,
it would have cried, 'I don't want to.
What are you urging me to do?
You are demanding the impossible!'
But the Cry, without pity, kept shaking its roots
and shouting, 'Away, let go of the earth, walk!'

It shouted in this way for thousands of eons;
and lo! as a result of desire and struggle,
life escaped the motionless tree and was liberated.

Animals appeared – worms –
making themselves at home in water and mud.
'We're just fine,' they said.
'We have peace and security; we're not budging!'

But the terrible Cry
hammered itself pitilessly into their loins.
'Leave the mud, stand up,
give birth to your betters!'
'We don't want to! We can't!'
'You can't, but I can. Stand up!'

And lo! After thousands of eons, man emerged,
trembling on his still unsolid legs.

NIKOS KAZANTZAKIS (1885-1957)

A Relationship

This uneluctable relatedness, this being held by something to which one's whole life is response . . . is the reality to which the language of 'God' points. To speak of 'God' is to refer neither, on the one hand, to an existence outside one's experience, nor, on the other, simply to one's own way of looking at the world. It is to acknowledge a relationship, a confrontation at the heart of one's very constitution as a human being, of which one is compelled to say, in existential terms, 'This is it. This is the most real thing in the world, that which is ultimately and inescapably true . . .'

We can say that, however much this awareness seems to come from within, from the ground of our very being, it confronts us also with an otherness to which we can only respond as 'I' to 'Thou'.

J. A. T. ROBINSON (1919-1983)

Only Seeds

A new shop opened up in the village. A woman went in and found God behind the counter.

'What are you selling here?'

'Everything you could possibly wish for.'

'Oh good. I'll have happiness, wisdom, love, freedom from fear, and peace, please. Oh, and for everyone.'

'Sorry, you got it wrong. I'm not selling any fruits. Only seeds.'

ANON

Disappearing God

Odd how he changes. When I was very young, I thought of God as a great blank thing, rather like the sky . . . all friendliness and protectiveness and fondness for little children . . . It was the great big blank egg of the sky that I loved and felt so safe and happy with. It went with a sense of being curled up. Perhaps I felt I was inside the egg.

Later it was different, it was when I first started to look at spiders . . . There is a spider called *Amaurobius* which has its young in the late summer, and then it dies when the frosts begin, and the young spiders live through the cold by eating their mother's dead body . . . God *was* those spiders which I watched in the light of my electric torch on summer nights. There was a wonderfulness, a separateness, it was the divine to see those spiders living their extraordinary lives.

Later on in adolescence it all became confused with emotion. I thought that God was Love, a big sloppy love that drenched the world with big wet kisses and made everything all right. I felt myself transformed, purified, glorified . . .

I loved God, I was in love with God, and the world was full of the power of love. There was a lot of God at that time.

Afterwards he became less, he got drier and pettier and more like an official who made rules. I had to watch my step with him. He was a kind of bureaucrat making checks and counterchecks . . . I stopped loving him and began to find him depressing.

Then he receded altogether, he became something that the women did, a sort of female activity, though very occasionally I met him again, most often in country churches when I was alone and suddenly he would be there. He was different once more in those meetings. He wasn't an official any longer. He was something rather lost and pathetic . . . I felt sorry for him . . .

Later on again he was simply gone, he was nothing but an intellectual fiction, an old hypothesis, a piece of literature.

Iris Murdoch (b.1919)

Living without God

God as a working hypothesis in morals, politics, or science, has been surmounted and abolished; and the same thing has happened in philosophy and religion . . . For the sake of intellectual honesty, that working hypothesis should be dropped, or as far as possible eliminated . . .

We cannot be honest unless we recognize that we have to live in the world *etsi deus non daretur*. And this is just what we do recognize – before God! God himself compels us to recognize it. So our coming of age leads us to a true recognition of our situation before God. God would have us know that we must live as men who manage our lives without him. The God who is with us is the God who forsakes us (Mark 15:34). The God who lets us live in the world without the working hypothesis of God is the God before whom we stand continually. Before God and with God we live without God. God lets himself be pushed out of the world on to the cross. He is weak and powerless in the world, and that is precisely the way, the only way, in which he is with us and helps us. Matt. 8:17 makes it quite clear that Christ helps us, not by virtue of his omnipotence, but by virtue of his weakness and suffering . . .

Man's religiosity makes him look in his distress to the power of God in the world: God is the *deus ex machina*. The Bible directs man to God's powerlessness and suffering; only the suffering God can help . . .

To be a Christian does not mean to be religious in a particular way, to make something of oneself (a sinner, a penitent, or a saint) on the basis of some method or other, but to be a man – not a type of man, but the man that Christ creates in us. It is not the religious act that makes the Christian, but participation in the sufferings of God in the secular life.

DIETRICH BONHOEFFER (1906-1945)

3 GOD CLOSE AT HAND

Scripture Reading

The Lord is my shepherd,
he provides all I need
in the rich grassland
where he lets me feed.
He brings me to water,
my life to renew;
he guides me on true paths,
because he is true.

I walk through the darkness,
with nothing to fear;
his right hand protects me
when danger is near.
He lays me a table,
in spite of my foes;
he fills me with gladness,
my cup overflows.

Each day he is goodness,
each day he's my song;
I live in his household
the whole of life long.
The Lord is my shepherd,
he provides all I need
in the rich grassland
where he lets me feed.

PSALM 23 (22)

Gently Holding Hands

The leaves are falling, falling as from far,
as though above were withering farthest gardens;
they fall with a denying attitude,
and night by night, down into solitude,
the heavy earth falls far from every star.
We are all falling. This hand's falling too –
all have this falling sickness none withstands.
And yet there's one whose gently-holding hands
this universal falling can't fall through.

R. M. RILKE (1875-1926)

God With Us

Late have I loved you, beauty ever old and ever new!
Late have I loved you!
You were within and I was without, and searched there for you,
running after all the beautiful things you made.
You were with me, but I was not with you,
held back by the things which should have led me to you.
But you called and called, and broke through my deafness.
You shone your light and overcame my blindness.
Your fragrance enveloped and overwhelmed me.
Your taste left me hungering and thirsting for you.
Your touch left me burning for your embrace.

ST AUGUSTINE 354-430
TRS. H. J. RICHARDS

Enveloped in Love

Before I was born your love enveloped me.
You turned nothing into substance, and created me.

Who etched out my frame? Who poured
me into a vessel and moulded me?
Who breathed a spirit into me? Who opened
the womb of the Underworld and extracted me?
Who has guided me from youth-time until now,
taught me knowledge, and cared wondrously for me?

Truly, I am nothing but clay within your hand.
It is you, not I, who have really fashioned me.
I confess my sin to you, and do not say
that a serpent intrigued and tempted me.
How can I conceal from you my faults, since
before I was born your love enveloped me?

SOLOMON IBN GABIROL (1021-1056)

Love Was His Meaning

Wouldest thou wit thy Lord's meaning in this thing?
Wit it well: love was his meaning.
Who sheweth it thee? Love.
What sheweth he thee? Love.
Wherefore sheweth he it thee? For love . . .
And I saw full surely in this and in all,
that ere God made us, he loved us;
which love was never slacked, ne never shall.
And in his love he hath done all his works:
and in this love he hath made
all things profitable to us:
and in this love our life is everlasting.
In our making we had beginning:
but the love wherein he made us
was in him fro without beginning.
In which love we have our beginning.
And all this shall we see in God without end.

JULIAN OF NORWICH (1342-1416)

God Loveth It

I saw that (God) is to us all thing that is good
and comfortable to our help.
He is our clothing, that for love wrappeth us . . .
that he maie never leave us . . .
He shewed a little thing,
the quantitie of a hasel-nutt,
lying in the palme of my hand,
and it was as round as a ball.
I looked theron with the eie of my understanding,
and thought, 'What may this be?'
and it was answered generallie thus:
'It is all that is made.'
I marvelled how it might last:
for me thought it might sodenlie
have fallen to naught for litlenes.
And I answered in my understanding,
'It lasteth, and ever shall:
for God loveth it.
And so hath all thing being by the love of God.'

JULIAN OF NORWICH (1342-1416)

In the Likeness of God

Moses received from God 613 commandments

David reduced them to eleven:
> In order to live on God's holy hill,
>> Live a blameless life
>> Do what is right
>> Speak the truth from your heart
>> Keep malice from your tongue
>> Do not wrong a friend
>> Do not slander your neighbour
>> Disdain the godless
>> Honour all those who fear God
>> Keep your word whatever it costs
>> Take no interest on loans
>> Take no bribe against the innocent (*Psalm 15(14)*)

Micah reduced them to three:
> He has shown you what is good:
>> Act justly
>> Love mercy
>> Walk humbly with your God (*Micah 6:8*)

Isaiah reduced them to two:
> Thus says the Lord:
>> Keep to justice
>> Do what is right (*Isaiah 56:1*)

Amos reduced them to one:
> The Lord says this to Israel:
>> Seek me and live (*Amos 5:4*)

Rabbi Akiba said that the Law's most important principle
is contained in the command:
> Love your neighbour as yourself: I am the Lord (*Leviticus 19:18*)

But Rabbi Ben Azai taught a greater principle:
> When God created man, he created him in the likeness of God
> (*Genesis 1:27*)

MISHNAH (2ND CENTURY)

God Gracious

If an example be required to upset the theory that advancing years destroy our belief in Santa Claus, I beg most modestly to present myself as an exception.

What has happened to me has been the very reverse of what appears to be the experience of most of my friends. Instead of dwindling to a point, Santa Claus has grown larger and larger in my life until he fills almost the whole of it. It happened in this way. As a child I was faced with a phenomenon requiring explanation; I hung up at the end of my bed an empty stocking, which in the morning had become a full stocking. I had done nothing to produce the things that filled it. I had not worked for them, or made them or helped to make them. I had not even been good – far from it. And the explanation was that a certain being, whom people called Santa Claus, was benevolently disposed towards me.

Of course most people who talk about these things get into a state of some mental confusion by attaching tremendous importance to the name of the entity. We called him Santa Claus because everybody called him Santa Claus; but the name of a God is a mere human label. His real name may have been Williams. It may have been the Archangel Uriel. What we believed was that a certain benevolent agency did give us those toys for nothing.

And, as I say, I believe it still. I have merely extended the idea. Then I only wondered who put the toys in the stocking; now I wonder who put the stocking by the bed, and the bed in the room, and the room in the house, and the house on the planet, and the planet in the void. Once I only thanked Santa Claus for a few dolls and crackers, now I thank him for stars and street faces and wine and the great sea. Once I thought it delightful and astonishing to find a present so big that it only went halfway into the stocking. Now I am delighted and astonished every morning to find a present so big that it takes two stockings to hold it, and then leaves a great deal outside; it is the large and preposterous present of myself, as to the origin of which I can afford no suggestion except that Santa Claus gave it to me in a fit of peculiarly fantastic goodwill.

G. K. CHESTERTON (1874-1936)

Incarnation

Our commonwealth is in heaven,
and from it we await a Saviour,
the Lord Jesus Christ,
who will change our lowly body
to be like his glorious body,
by the power which enables him
to subject all things to himself.
(*Philippians 3:20-21*)

From this text notice briefly three things.

1. First, our commonwealth or citizenship is in heaven. Whatever else that means, it means that heaven is where we already belong . . . If the Christian holds a passport, it is not a passport to get him *to* heaven at death, but a passport *from* heaven to live within this world as the representative and ambassador of a foreign style of life . . .

2. The second point is that the Christian hope is not so much a hope *for* heaven as a hope *from* heaven. The heart of the Christian hope is not that the housing committee of the Celestial City Council moves us from this slum to that 'other country' . . . but rather that the life of God (heaven) will so penetrate the life of man (earth) that God's will shall be done on earth as it is in heaven. Of that movement from God to man, the Incarnation is the pledge, the Parousia is the promise . . .

3. But, thirdly, what is the relation of the new to the old? . . . The gospel of the Reign of God is not the salvaging of souls from a mass of perdition, but 'the redemption of the body', that is, the reintegration of the whole man in all his relationships, physical and spiritual, in a new solidarity which creates personality rather than destroys it. And the gospel goes on to insist that this new man has already been created, in the body of Christ, and that within the life of the Church, the new God-given structure of existence has even now begun to penetrate and transform this world . . .

For risen men, whose real death is behind them, the moment of physical death can no longer be the focus of their gaze. Our gaze as Christians is not at death, nor even beyond it at the skies, but at God's world (this world) from the other side of it. And from there where Christ is seated at the right hand of God, 'O death, where is thy victory? O grave, where is thy sting?'

J. A. T. ROBINSON (1919-1983)

More Present Than Ever

The Lisbon earthquake has shaken believers the world over.
The more sadistically minded are interpreting it
as my retribution on a wicked world.
I wish such people
would stop calling themselves believers.
They don't know the first thing about me.

The more thoughtful are asking
how I could allow such a thing.
Why didn't I prevent it?
But, omnipotent as I am,
'allowing' and 'preventing' is not within my power.
I have created a vulnerable world
where fire not only warms people but also burns them,
where water not only slakes their thirst
but also drowns them.
Who but plastic robots could live in a world
that was otherwise?

What people need to understand is
that in disasters of this kind, I am not absent,
but more present than ever.
I am not the God whom philosophers and theologians
call *impassibilis* (impassive?) or *apathetos* (apathetic?).
I am the God seen in Jesus,
more present (and heartbroken) in his tragic death
even than in his radiant life.
And more anxious than ever in 'bad times'
than in 'good times'
that people reveal my presence
in the love they show for each other.

'How can anyone find God in this situation?' people say.
How can anyone help fish find the ocean?

God's Diary
H. J. RICHARDS (B.1921)

The Nearest Thou

Who is God? Not in the first place an abstract belief in God, in his omnipotence etc. That is not a genuine experience of God, but a partial extension of the world. Encounter with Jesus Christ. The experience that a transformation of all human life is given in the fact that 'Jesus is there only for others'. His 'being there for others' is the experience of transcendence. It is only this 'being there for others', maintained till death, that is the ground of his omnipotence, omniscience, and omnipresence . . . Our relation to God is not a 'religious' relationship to the highest, most powerful, and best Being imaginable – that is not authentic transcendence – but our relation to God is a new life in 'existence for others', through participation in the being of Jesus. The transcendental is not infinite and unattainable tasks, but the neighbour who is within reach in any given situation. God in human form . . . 'the man for others', and therefore the Crucified, the man who lives out of the transcendent . . .

The church is the church only when it exists for others. To make a start, it should give away all its property to those in need . . . The church must share in the secular problems of ordinary human life, not dominating, but helping and serving. It must tell men of every calling what it means to live in Christ, to exist for others.

DIETRICH BONHOEFFER (1906-1945)

A World Transformed

If I love the world as it is,
I am already changing it:
a first fragment of the world has been changed,
and that is my own heart.
Through this first fragment
the light of God, his goodness and his love,
penetrate into the midst
of his anger and sorrow and darkness,
dispelling them as the smile on a human face
dispels the lowered brows and the frowning gaze.

PETRU DUMITRIU

God Revealed

All things search until they find
God through the gateway of thy mind.

Highest star and humblest clod
turn home through thee to God.

When thou rejoicest in the rose
blissful from earth to heaven she goes;

Upon they bosom summer seas
escape from their captivities;

Within thy sleep the sightless eyes
of night revisage Paradise;

In thy soft awe yon mountain high
to his creator draweth nigh;

This lonely tarn, reflecting thee,
returneth to eternity;

And thus in thee the circuit vast
is rounded and complete at last,

And at last, through thee revealed
to God, what time and space concealed.

EDITH ANNE STEWART

Human Form Divine

To Mercy, Pity, Peace and Love
all pray in their distress;
and to these virtues of delight
return their thankfulness.

For Mercy, Pity, Peace and Love
is God, our father dear,
and Mercy, Pity, Peace and Love
is Man, his child and care.

For Mercy has a human heart,
Pity a human face,
and Love, the human form divine,
and Peace the human dress.

Then every man, of every clime,
that prays in his distress,
prays to the human form divine,
Love, Mercy, Pity, Peace.

And all must love the human form,
in heathen, Turk or Jew;
where Mercy, Love and Pity dwell
there God is dwelling too.

WILLIAM BLAKE (1757-1827)

The God I Need

Don't need no god.
Don't need no eternal paternal god.
Don't need no reassuringly protective
    good and evil in perspective – god.
Don't need no imported distorted
    inflated updated
    holy roller, save your soul, or
    anaesthetisingly opiate – gods.
Don't need no 'all creatures that on earth do dwell'
    be good or you'll go to hell – god.
Don't need no Hare Krishna Hare Krishna
    Hail Mary Hail Mary – god.
Don't need no televised circumcised
    incessant incandescent – god.
Don't need no god.
I need human beings.
I need some kind
of love.
I need you.

ANDREW DARLINGTON

4 JESUS WORD OF GOD

Scripture Readings

If he were no more than a prophet,
he'd have heard God's voice in a dream,
he'd have seen God's face in a vision,
he'd have seen what all prophets have seen.

But he was much more than a prophet,
he heard so much more than a dream,
he saw so much more than a vision:
he had been where no other has been.

He was at home in God's presence,
he could treat God's house as his;
he heard and he saw God quite plainly,
and through him we know God as he is.

BOOK OF NUMBERS 12:6-8 AND GOSPEL OF JOHN 1:18

He spoke the language
    both of earth and of heaven,
    but if he had had no love
    it would have been so much old iron.

He was a prophet who could explain
    all the wonders and secrets of God.

He was wise with all knowledge.

He had faith so complete
    he could have moved mountains,
    but if he had had no love
    it would all have been worthless.

He gave everything he possessed,
    even his life,
    as a martyr for what he believed,
    but if he had been without love
    it would have gone for nothing.

He was never in a hurry
    and was always kindness itself.

He never envied anybody at all
    and never boasted about himself.

He was never snobbish
    or rude, or selfish.

He didn't keep on talking
    about the wrong things other people do;
    remembering the good things
    was happiness enough for him.

He was tough –
    he could face anything.

And he never lost trust in God,
    or in men and women.

He never lost hope.

And he never gave in.

St Paul to the Corinthians I 13:1-7
trs. A. T. Dale

God For Us

If the subject of theology were God alone,
enthroned above the cherubim,
then indeed the truth would not alter,
and changes in theology would prove merely
that we were dealing with passing human ideas
masquerading as supernatural science.
But Christian theology is about truth incarnate –
and it must change with the world
in which the truth has to be made flesh.
For the Christian, truth is always concrete.
Jesus Christ is 'the same
yesterday, today and forever'
only by being the contemporary of each generation,
and therefore different for each generation.
The Christ of the fifth, or the fifteenth,
or the nineteenth century
is not Christ for us today.
Far more than theologians have been wont to acknowledge,
Christianity is always changing,
because the world is always changing;
for it is about God *ad hominem*, God *pro nobis* –
God related to man, God for us.

J. A. T. ROBINSON (1919-1983)

Why He Came

Dear Reverend God,

Your private research commission has prepared its final report.
As chairperson I must inform you
 that we are unanimously against your project
 and for the following reasons:

It's dangerous for your son to become a human being:
 he could be hungry, thirsty, suffer or even be killed.
But if you insist, we suggest a few changes and some delay:

Jesus must be born from a married woman:
 nobody will believe the story of Mary and the angel.
Or he should appear on earth as an adult:
 why waste all those growing up years?
Whether Jesus is a boy or a girl,
 50% of the people will feel discriminated against.
The birth in a stable is ridiculous:
 our commission prefers a palace.
Shepherds shouldn't be involved:
 they are scorned even by the middle class.
Galilee is a remote province, little esteemed:
 Jesus won't find the right kind of apostles there.
Transportation system is too slow yet:
 It's a long walk from Nazareth to Jerusalem.
Sound systems don't exist yet:
 too few people will hear Jesus' message.
But the most compelling reason against your plan
 is that it has never been done before.

And God said:

Thanks to all the members of your commission.
You are very intelligent, and you have discovered
 very valuable reasons against my project.
But what do your *hearts* tell you?

Dear Reverend God,

You asked us for a study
based on scientific facts and rational analysis.
The *heart* reasons were not part of our mandate.
You are the specialist about the love questions.

Good, said God.
I'm glad you feel like this.
Then, let's go for it.

FR. RENÉ FUMOLEAU

Christ The Saviour

Soul of Jesus, make me holy;
Christ's own body, be my saving;
blood of Jesus, slake my thirsting;
water from your pierced side, wash me.

May your Passion give me comfort;
o good Jesus, hear my prayer;
let your wounds protect and hide me,
never to be parted from you.

From my enemies defend me;
at my dying moment call me;
summon me into your presence,
to be with your saints for ever.

POPE JOHN XXII (1249-1334)
TRS. H. J. RICHARDS (B. 1921)

Christ the Dancer

I danced in the morning when the world was begun,
and I danced in the moon and the stars and the sun,
and I came down from heaven and I danced on the earth;
at Bethlehem I had my birth.

    Dance, then, wherever you may be,
    I am the Lord of the dance, said he,
    and I'll lead you all, wherever you may be,
    and I'll lead you all in the dance, said he.

I danced for the scribe and the pharisee,
but they would not dance and they wouldn't follow me;
I danced for the fishermen, for James and John –
they came with me and the dance went on.

I danced on the Sabbath and I cured the lame:
the holy people said it was a shame;
they whipped and they stripped and they hung me on high,
and they left me there on a cross to die.

I danced on a Friday when the sky turned black –
it's hard to dance with the devil on your back;
they buried my body and they thought I'd gone,
but I am the dance, and I still go on.

They cut me down and I leapt up high;
I am the life that'll never, never die;
I'll live in you if you'll live in me;
I am the Lord of the dance, said he.

SYDNEY CARTER (B. 1925)

The Godsend

What does the story of the Virgin Birth mean?
It means that, of all the human race,
Jesus is the one who comes to us from God.
From what his disciples had experienced of him,
in his life and teaching and death and resurrection,
they concluded that
of all the divine births of which they had read
here was the one which was most truly God-given,
that this was most truly God's gift through and through.
He is not merely Godlike or the noblest of men:
they had discovered him to be the complete expression of God,
a non-distorting mirror of God at work,
one who brings God utterly.
They had seen that his whole life is of God,
that his being is rooted in God alone,
that he is not 'of the word' but 'of love'.
In him they had seen something
of the final mystery of life itself:
they had touched rock.
God shone through him,
and of such a person all you could say was
that his life was fathered in Mary
by the very Spirit of God.
His birth and life could not be thought of
simply as biological events;
his significance lay much deeper.
He was the beginning of a new Israel,
with a new Sarah for his mother,
and a future only from God.

H. J. RICHARDS (B.1921)

45

All of a Man

Jesus: God does not cheat.

Judas: I don't understand – ?

Jesus: The son of man must be a man. He must be all of a man. He must pass water like a man. He must get hungry and feel tired and sick and lonely. He must laugh. He must cry. He cannot be other than a man, or else God has *cheated*.

Judas: But Jesus – if –

Jesus: (*urgently*): And so my Father in heaven will abandon me to myself. And if my head aches he will not lift the ache out of it. And if my stomach rumbles he will not clean out my bowels. And if a snake curls into my thoughts, then the fang will be in my mind. If I were to have *no* doubt I would be *other than a man*.
(*Pause*)
And God does not cheat.
(*Pause*)

Judas: Then how shall we know?

Jesus: By what you see. By what you hear. How else?

DENNIS POTTER (1935-1994)

This is Man

This was the look of him? This down-to-earth man?
This convinces me. None of the flimsy faces
the painters put on him. This man never arrived
at resurrection without a hard won fight,
nor was half-air before he achieved ascension.
With *him*, he took a look of the earth he lay in –
rock, and a little soil, and old olive roots –
a sturdy, serene man, common sense in a riddle.
He looks like his talk, before it was pared by parsons,
spun into sermons, and so on, transtabulated
into theology. This man is marvellous –
death instinct with life, life at peace.
This is man.

They say he will judge me. I'm convinced.
I am judged already. I stand before him, knowing
that like each man I am my own disaster.
He knows I know. He will be merciful.
This man looks like all that I ask of God –
I can call him both me and master.

JAMES BRABAZON (B. 1923)

A Proper Man

I saw the grass, I saw the trees
and the boats along the shore;
I saw the shapes of many things
I had only sensed before;
and I saw the faces of men more clearly
than if I had never been blind,
the lines of envy around their lips,
and the greed and hate in their eyes;
and I turned away, yes I turned away,
for I had seen the perfect face of a real and proper man,
the man who'd brought me from the dark
into light, where life began.

I hurried then away from town
to a quiet and lonely place;
I found a clear, unruffled pool
and I gazed upon my face;
and I saw the image of me more clearly
than if I had never been blind,
the lines of envy around the lips,
and the greed and hate in the eyes;
and I turned away, yes I turned away,
for I had seen the perfect face of a real and proper man,
the man who'd brought me from the dark
into light, where life began.

I made my way back into town,
to the busy, crowded streets,
the shops and stalls and alley-ways,
to the squalor and the heat;
and I saw the faces of men more clearly
than if I had never been blind,
the lines of sorrow around their lips,
and the child looking out from their eyes;
and I turned to them, yes I turned to them,
remembering the perfect face of a real and proper man,
the man who'd brought me from the dark
into light, where life began.

ESTELLE WHITE

Our Man

When they came wi' a host to take our man,
his smile was good to see,
'First let these go,' quoth our godly Fere,
'or I'll see ye damned,' says he.

Aye, he sent us through the crossed high spears,
and the scorn of his laugh rang free,
'Why took ye not me when I walked about
alone in the town?' says he.

O we drank his hale in the good red wine
when we last made company,
no capon priest was the godly Fere,
but a man o' men was he.

ANON

Our Lord The Man

Down Huddersfield Road goes a lonely man:
all night at his loom, he walks home through the gloom,
no home, only a room.
Down Huddersfield Road goes a lonely man:
face tired and worn, in the strange light of dawn,
Lord, he looks so forlorn.
Down Huddersfield Road goes a lonely man.

O you who seek God in the skies, you waste your chances:
you will not recognise his advances.
O you who seek God in the skies, in vain you labour:
better lower your eyes and look at your neighbour.

Down Huddersfield Road goes a lonely man:
all night at his loom, he walks home through the gloom,
no home, only a room.
Down Huddersfield Road goes our Lord, the man:
face tired and worn, in the strange light of dawn,
Lord, you look so forlorn.
Down Huddersfield Road goes our Lord, the man.

PÈRE AIMÉ DUVAL

Christ Now

Christ has no body on earth but yours,
no hands but yours, no feet but yours.
Yours are the eyes through which his compassion
must look out on the world.
Yours are the feet with which Christ
is to go about doing good.
Yours are the hands with which
he now gives his blessing.

St Teresa of Avila (1515-1582)

The Dignity of Human Beings

A proposal was made at the United Nations
that all Scriptures of all the religions in the world be revised.
Anything in them that would lead to intolerance
or cruelty or bigotry
should be deleted.
Anything that would in any way
be against the dignity and welfare of human beings
should be dropped.

News reporters wanted to know who made the proposal.
They were told it was Jesus Christ.
They all rushed to him to ask for further details.
He said, 'It's very simple.
Like the Sabbath, the Scriptures were made for man,
not man for the Scriptures.'

Anthony de Mello (d. 1987)

Hevene King

Of on that is so fayr and bright
    Velut maris stella,
Brighter than the day is light
    Parens et puella;
Ic crie to thee, thou see to me,
Levedy, preye thi Sone for me
    Tam pia
That ic mote come to thee,
    Maria.

Al this worlde was for-lore
    Eva peccatrice
Tyl our Lorde was y-bore
    De te genetrice;
With ave it went away
Thuster nyth, and comz the day
    Salutis;
The welle springeth ut of the
    Virtutis.

Levedy, flour of alle thing
    Rosa sine spina,
Thu bere Jhesu, hevene king
    Gratia divina;
Of alle thu ber'st the pris,
Levedy, quene of paradys
    Electa;
Mayde milde, moder es
    Effecta.

MEDIEVAL HYMN TO MARY
ANON

For Love of Me

Let me love thee, O Christ,
in thy first coming,
when thou wast made man, for love of men,
and for love of me.

Let me love thee, O Christ,
in thy second coming,
when with an inconceivable love
thou standest and knockest at the door,
and wouldest enter into the souls of men,
and into mine.

Plant in my soul, O Christ,
thy likeness of love,
that when by death thou callest,
it may be ready
and burning
to come unto thee.

ERIC MILNER-WHITE

5 SPIRIT OF CHRIST

Scripture Readings

What I am about to do on your behalf
will show the whole world the sort of God I am,
and every nation will recognize my power.
I am going to rescue you from your enslavement
and bring you home to the land where you belong.
I am going to pour fresh water over you
to wash you clean from all that defiles you
and cleanse you from the false gods you have followed.
I am going to give you a new heart, and a new Spirit:
a sensitive heart to replace your frozen one,
and my own Spirit to guide you in my ways.
Then you will truly be my people,
and I will be your God.

THE PROPHET EZEKIEL 36:23-28

God's own love has been poured into our hearts:
his Holy Spirit has made a home in us.
It is not a Spirit that ties us to God like slaves,
but the Spirit of God's own Son,
enabling us to cry out with him, 'Abba, Our Father.'
What this Spirit produces in us is love and joy,
peace, patience, kindness and goodness,
fidelity, gentleness and self-control.
If we live in the Spirit of such a Christ,
our behaviour should show it.

ST PAUL TO THE ROMANS 8:5-15
AND GALATIANS 5:22-26

God's Spirit is in my heart;
he has called me and set me apart;
this is what I have to do:

> He's sent me to give the good news to the poor,
> tell prisoners that they are prisoners no more,
> tell blind people that they can see,
> and set the downtrodden free,
> and go tell everyone
> the news that the kingdom of God has come.

Just as the Father sent me,
so I'm sending you out to be
my witnesses throughout the world.

By dying I'm going away,
but I'll be with you every day
as the Spirit of love in your heart.

Don't worry what you have to say;
don't worry, because on that day
God's Spirit will speak in your heart.

THE GOSPELS OF LUKE 4:18, JOHN 20:21 AND 16:16, MARK 13:11.

Come Holy Spirit

Holy Spirit, come, we pray,
and a single heavenly ray
of thy Light to us impart.

Come thou Father of the poor,
come thou Gift which will endure,
come thou Brightness of the heart.

Of Consolers thou art best,
in our hearts the dearest Guest,
dearest Friend through all the years.

After work our Rest at night,
Shade against the sun's fierce light,
Solace when we are in tears.

Of all lights thou loveliest Light,
shine on us and chase the night
from the crannies of our soul.

Nothing is more certain than
without thee there is in man
nothing innocent or whole.

Cleanse us of each sinful stain,
soak our dryness with thy rain,
soothe and heal what suffers pain.

Unbend fast the bigot's brain,
fan all fires that start to wane,
bring the lost sheep home again.

Grant thy seven-fold Gift to those
in whose heart thy mercy flows,
those with faith and trust in thee.

Grant them virtue's rich reward,
grant them death in Christ their Lord,
grant them joy eternally.

STEPHEN LANGTON (1160-1228)
TRS. PETER DE ROSA (B. 1932)

The Kiss of God

The Holy Spirit is the kiss and poetry of God.
He inspires the prophets, the poets and the artists.
He animates the whole of creation.
He makes it possible for creatures to become aware of God . . .
He is the realization in space and time
of the all-enveloping presence of God.
Because of this awareness of God's presence,
we become deified . . .
Without the Holy Spirit
we are strangers and far from God . . .
It is he who searches the deep things of God
and reveals them to us . . .
He sings and wants to make us sing
in joy and wonder at the discovery of God
and of all things in God.

ARCHBISHOP JOSEPH RAYA

God's Love Let Loose

On the cross, the Father gives up his Son,
and the Son accepts being given up.
The Father suffers the grief of the loss of his Son.
The Son suffers the loss of his own life,
and even more deeply the abandonment by his Father:
'My God, my God, why have you forsaken me?'
This deep suffering penetrates the very being of God.
In a very literal sense, God is suffering.
Yet while each is suffering the loss of the other,
they have never been so deeply united in one love.
In their common loving will
to save the world regardless of the cost,
what is revealed is the Holy Spirit,
who is the Love of the Father and the Son.
At Jesus' death his Spirit, God's Love
is let loose on the world.
The Love between Father and Son
is released into creation
and begins to bring about redemption.

ELIZABETH A. JOHNSON

Spirit of Peace

Father, at the Supper, Jesus said:
Peace I leave with you;
my peace I give to you;
not as the world gives I give to you.
The peace of Christ left with us, Father,
is the peace of the Dove,
the gentle presence of the holy Spirit.
In Christ you blessed your people with peace,
because in him we find the Spirit
of love and reconciliation.
Over the troubled waters of his disciples' hearts,
the risen Christ said, 'Peace, be still!'
and the winds fell and the waves ceased
and at last they found themselves to be men of peace.
Whatever tribulations they had in the world,
in Christ they had peace,
for he had overcome the world.
The risen Christ breathed on them;
and borne upon his breath
was the Dove of your divine forgiveness;
and they blessed you, Father, for your grace and peace.
Father, may the Whitsuntide Christ
breathe his Spirit of peace on me,
and make me an instrument of your peace.
In the holy Spirit, Father,
I have calmed and quieted my soul
like a child quieted at its mother's breast;
like a child that is quieted is my soul.

PETER DE ROSA (B.1932)

Spirit of Jesus

The concept of the Holy Spirit has been misused in modern times
both by the official Church and by pious individuals.
When holders of high office in the Church
did not know how to justify their own claims to infallibility,
they pointed to the Holy Spirit.
When theologians did not know how to justify
a particular doctrine, a dogma or a biblical term,
they appealed to the Holy Spirit.
When mild or wild fanatics did not know
how to justify their subjectivist whims,
they invoked the Holy Spirit . . .
The Holy Spirit was made a substitute
for cogency, authorization, plausibility,
intrinsic credibility, objective discussion.
It was not so in the early Church . . .

Perceptible and yet not perceptible,
invisible yet powerful,
real like the energy-charged air, the wind, the storm,
as important for life as the air we breathe:
this is how people in ancient times
imagined the 'Spirit' and God's invisible working . . .
The Spirit is no other than God himself . . .
He is not a third party,
not a thing between God and us,
but God's personal closeness to us . . .
And since God himself acted in Jesus,
the Spirit could be understood also
as the Spirit of the Jesus who is exalted to God . . .
Jesus can even himself be understood as Spirit:
Paul even says, 'The Lord is the Spirit' (*2 Cor. 3:17*) . . .
In the Spirit, therefore, the exalted Christ is present . . .
The phrases 'in the Spirit' and 'in Christ',
or even 'the Spirit in us' and 'Christ in us'
can run parallel, and in practice be interchanged.

HANS KÜNG (B. 1928)

Sharing Christ's Spirit

Many people think of the Spirit
as a kind of ghostly third person
who, they are told, is of vital importance
to their spiritual lives,
but they can't quite see why.
Perhaps it would help if we realized
that the Holy Spirit is nothing other
than the Spirit of love in which Jesus lived his whole life,
and which he yearned to share with everyone.
He did this when he died.
It was only in his death that Jesus,
whose whole life had spoken of God,
became the Word of God so clearly
that no one could any longer be mistaken
about what God is like.
God is like this figure on the cross;
he totally accepts and suffers
the worst that people can do, and still forgives.
So in death, Jesus, the man who is for others,
reveals that God is like that from all eternity,
totally for others,
totally on our side
against the forces that would destroy us.
Indeed it is only because of that,
that the forces of evil are neutralized and transformed.
Because life is always stronger than death,
and love has a power that evil cannot match.
It's in this Spirit that Jesus lived his whole life.
His death meant that, instead of sharing that Spirit
with only the few that spoke to him and heard him,
he was now free of all limitations
and could pour out that Spirit
on all who understood the meaning of his death.
And those who drank of that Spirit
said that they would never thirst for anything else.
It had become like a living fountain of water
in their own hearts – this secret of living in God's own way.
To share the Spirit of Christ,
to live in the way he lived and died,
is to know God as he did.

H. J. RICHARDS (B.1921)

Light of the World

Father, you are Light
and in you there is no darkness at all.
You alone have immortality
and dwell in light so unapproachable
no one has ever seen you or can see you.
But in Christ, Father,
you lifted up the light of your countenance on us.
He is the Light of the world,
for he reflects the glory of your face,
the glory which is your holy Spirit.
In heaven the night is ended.
There is no need of lamp or sun or moon
because the Lamb is the lamp of the city
and your glory is its light.
And even here, Father, we are seeing this light
which comes into the world in Christ.
Death seemed to extinguish the light,
but your Spirit rekindled the Lamp
and it will shine for ever more.
Spirit of the risen Christ,
shine brightly on us
so we may walk as children of light
and have our long lost innocence restored to us.

PETER DE ROSA (B. 1932)

Pentecost is Today

What a joy for us to praise you, Lord,
and open wide the gates of our heart
to the wind and fire of your Spirit,
which fill the earth
with the immense newness of the Lord Jesus!

He it is who promised we would not be orphans
but experience consolation and strength
and inebriating joy in the glory of love,
through which the Spirit comes
to proclaim your splendour in our whole life,
teaching our lips and hearts to call you
'Father, God of all goodness.'

That is why, with the prophets,
fired with the power of the Spirit;
with the martyrs,
filled with the boldness of the Spirit;
with Mary and the apostles, and all who testify
that, for them, Pentecost is today,
we praise you and sing your glory.

PIERRE GRIOLET

6 FAITH AND HOPE

Scripture Reading

The heart of all religion is trust in God,
which makes our hope for the future a strong hope,
and makes us sure about God himself whom we cannot see,
and about the world which he made to be his world.

If we are to live in God's Way, we must trust God,
Which means trusting in Jesus who has made God real to us.
This allows us to be happy even when we have to face hard times,
knowing that hard times train us never to give in.
Never giving in is the secret of growing up,
and being grown-up (as Jesus was grown-up),
we look forward with high hope to the future.
We aren't dreaming; for God himself lives in us,
and our hearts are full to overflowing with his love.

THE LETTERS TO THE HEBREWS 11:1 AND THE ROMANS 5:1-5
TRS. BY A. T. DALE

Strong in Hope

Lord, we thank you for your gift of hope,
our strength in times of trouble.
Beyond the injustice of our time,
its cruelty and its wars,
we look forward to a world at peace
when men deal kindly with each other,
and no one is afraid.
Every bad deed delays its coming,
every good one brings it nearer.
May our lives be your witness,
so that future generations bless us.
May the day come, as the prophet taught,
when 'the sun of righteousness
will rise with healing in its wings.'
Help us to pray for it, to wait for it,
to work for it, and to be worthy of it.

JEWISH PRAYER FOR SABBATH MORNING

God's Promises

These are the promises of God
and the duties he lays on us for the building of his kingdom:

The wolf shall live with the lamb,
the leopard lie down with the kid,
the calf and young lion shall feed together,
and a little child shall lead them. (*Isaiah 11:6*)

A shoot shall grow from the broken tree of Jesse
and a branch shall spring from its roots.
The spirit of the Lord shall rest upon him,
the spirit of wisdom and understanding. (*Isaiah 11:1-2*)

No duty is more sacred than for man
to cherish that spark of the Messiah in his soul
and save it from extinction. (*Nachman of Bratzlav 1772-1811*)

The world is judged by the majority of its people,
and an individual is judged by the majority of his deeds.
Happy the man who performs a good deed:
that may tip the scales for him and the world. (*Mishnah 2nd century*)

It shall be said in that day: This is our God
for whom we waited that he might save us;
this is the Lord for whom we waited,
we will be glad and rejoice in his salvation. (*Isaiah 25:9*)

May his Kingdom come in your lifetime, and in your days,
and in the lifetime of all the family of Israel –
quickly and speedily may it come. (*Prayer for the dead*)

JEWISH SABBATH MORNING SERVICE

Despair is Indecent

The story of the Tower of Babel at first sight seems to embody a truth which belongs to the primitive stages of religion – the idea of a jealous God. In fact there is subtlety about the Myth which Man, no matter how sophisticated his thinking, would be foolhardy to ignore. The God who destroys the Tower of Babel is pronouncing judgement on the refusal of Man to accept his finiteness. The moral of Babel is threefold, and simple. Man is mortal – that is his fate; Man refuses to accept the limits of his mortality – that is his sin; Man's proudest achievements are reduced to dust and ashes – that is his punishment.

Every civilization is, in the eyes of God, a Tower of Babel . . . One by one these Towers of Babel crash to the ground when prodded by God's finger. Their foundations may be solid; it is their pinnacles that are unstable because they are constructed of earthly materials unable to withstand the force of the winds of Heaven.

So according to the Myth of Babel men are punished for their arrogant pride by being scattered across the face of the earth, unable to communicate with each other. The crashing of the Tower is the beginning of cacophony – meaningless sounds that produce only noises devoid of harmony or relationship . . .

The Myth of Babel describes a human condition redolent of confusion and totally without hope. And were it to stand alone in the Bible without a counterpart, then Man could only bow his head, acknowledge the truth of it, and abandon himself to whatever fate overtook him for the sin of claiming finality for his achievements. But there are no loose ends in the Bible – God always finishes his sentences though his words may seem intolerably far apart. There *is* a counterpart to Babel – Pentecost. Men gather in one place, are filled with the Spirit, and rediscover a universal language . . . The curse of Babel has been cancelled. Men are once again brothers because they are joined together in Christ who died and rose for all . . . Jesus has become a centre around which all men can cohere, reconciled in their conflicts and transformed from competitors into comrades. The infinite distance between God and Man, which Babel could not bridge, has not merely been spanned. It has been abolished by, in and through Jesus. . .

So Man has cause for hope. Despair is not merely inappropriate, but downright indecent in a world shot through with the reconciling power of God.

COLIN MORRIS (B. 1929)

67

An Act of Faith

A reading from the Holy Scriptures.

And it came to pass that there was a goose that laid a golden egg each day. And the wife of the farmer that owned the goose delighted in the riches that the eggs brought her. But being greedy, she could not wait patiently from day to day for her eggs. So she killed the goose in order to get all the eggs at once. And having killed it, she was left with a half-formed egg, and a dead goose that could lay no more.

This is the Word of the Lord.

An atheist read the text and scoffed: 'You call that the Word of God? A goose that lays golden eggs! It just goes to show how much credence you can give to this so-called God!'

A preacher read the text, and spent his life travelling through towns and villages zealously urging people to accept the fact that at some point in history God had created golden eggs.

A theologian read that the text and said: 'The Lord clearly tells us that there was a goose that laid golden eggs. If the Lord says this, then it must be true, no matter how absurd it appears to our poor human minds. As a matter of fact, archaeological studies give us some vague hints that there did exist, at some time in ancient history, a mysterious goose that did in fact lay golden eggs. We might ask how an egg, while not ceasing to be an egg, can at the same time be golden. No answer can be given to this, although different schools of religious thought have made attempts to explain it. But being a mystery that baffles the human mind, what is ultimately called for is an act of faith.'

ANTHONY DE MELLO (D. 1987)

Faith and Security

Show me the book of rules
the good boy said
I'll be obedient.

The rules of God
are in this Holy Book
the parson said.

But how can I
be sure that
you are right?

You can't be sure.

I have created you
in my own image.
Do you think that I

Crave for security?
Go out upon
a limb, the way I do:

Create a world,
be crucified,
and be obedient

Only to what you are.

Get thee behind me
Satan, the good boy said
I only want

To see the book of rules
the good boy said
to be obedient.

SYDNEY CARTER (B. 1925)

Coming of Age

At a meeting of the Jewish Council, the gathered fathers had discussed a motion for some time. They finally took a vote. All voted in favour of the motion. Except for one learned rabbi. He was so convinced that the unanimous decision of the rest was wrong, that he called on a tree to uproot itself to support him.

Surprisingly, the tree did so. The Council, however, ruled that in matters of law, trees cannot give evidence. With horror, the rabbi called on a river to stop and reverse its direction. The river did so. But the Council still ruled that, in matters of law, rivers cannot give evidence.

In desperation, the rabbi called on the *Bat Qol* (the Voice from Heaven) to intervene on his behalf. The Voice did so, and confirmed that the rabbi was right. The Council, consistent to the end, ruled that, in matters of law, Heaven itself cannot give evidence, and made its decision against the rabbi.

And God danced for joy that his children had defeated him, and so proved that they had grown up.

TALMUD (5TH CENTURY)

Maturity

A sheep found a hole in the fence and crept through it. He was so glad to get away. He wandered far and lost his way back.

Then he realized he was being followed by a wolf. He ran and ran, but the wolf kept chasing him, until the shepherd came and rescued him and carried him lovingly back to the fold.

And in spite of everyone's urgings to the contrary, the shepherd refused to nail up the hole in the fence.

ANTHONY DE MELLO (D. 1987)

Hope for Everyone

Should I celebrate the day of my birth?
Others know best – let them decide.
But that moment, the day they set me free
from the barbed wire of the prison-camp;
that hour not destined to arrive
did come in early March, in Siberian frost
bright with stars at high noon.
That hour I recited the blessing
not spoken since childhood.
Now I persuade myself: such an hour, such a day
will be bestowed at last on every human friend.
That festal day
will pass through every door
without the need to knock.

SAMUEL HALKIN (1897-1960)
TRS. FROM YIDDISH BY CHAIM STERN

You Shall Dance

You would know the secret of death.
But how shall you find it
unless you seek it in the heart of life?
The owl whose night-bound eyes are blind unto the day
cannot unveil the mystery of light.
If you would indeed behold the spirit of death,
open your heart wide unto the body of life.
For life and death are one,
even as the river and the sea are one.

In the depth of your hopes and desires
lies your silent knowledge of the beyond,
and like seeds dreaming beneath the snow
your heart dreams of spring.
Trust the dreams,
for in them is hidden the gate to eternity.
Your fear of death is but the trembling of the shepherd
when he stands before the king
whose hand is to be laid on him in honour.
Is the shepherd not joyful beneath his trembling,
that he shall wear the mark of the king?
Yet is he not more mindful of his trembling?

For what is it to die
but to stand naked in the wind and to melt into the sun?
And what is it to cease breathing
but to free the breath from its restless tides,
that it may rise and expand and seek God unencumbered?

Only when you drink from the river of silence
shall you indeed sing.
And when you have reached the mountain top,
then you shall begin to climb.
And when the earth shall claim your limbs,
then shall you truly dance.

KAHLIL GIBRAN (1883-1931)

Trustfulness

What do our rabbis teach us about death? We know nothing of what is beyond the grave, and surely, the rabbis were strict about those who wanted to know what no man is given to know. But they taught us to pray: Blessed art thou, O Lord, who art a true friend to those who sleep in the dust. The rabbis taught us to pray: Blessed art thou, O Lord, who quickenest the dead. We do not die into the grave, we die into the eternity of God.

IGNAZ MAYBAUM (1897-1976)

Safe Lodging

May he support us all day long,
till the shadows lengthen and the evening comes,
and the busy world is hushed,
and the fever of life is over,
and our work is done.
Then in his mercy,
may he give us safe lodging,
and a holy rest and peace at last.

JOHN HENRY NEWMAN (1801-1890)

7 PRAYER AND PRAISE

Scripture Reading

Praise the Lord in the universe
    his sanctuary
by a radio signal 100,000 million light-years away
Praise him in his stars
    and his interstellar spaces
Praise him in his galaxies
    and his intergalactic spaces
Praise him in his atoms
    and in his subatomic spaces
Praise him with violin and flute
    and with saxophone
Praise him with clarinet and horn
      with cornet and trombone
      with alto sax and trumpet
Praise him with viola and cello
    with piano and harpsichord
Praise him with blues and jazz
    and with symphony orchestra
with spirituals of black peoples
    and with Beethoven's Fifth
    with guitars and marimbas
Praise him with record players
    and with tape recorders
Everything that breathes praise the Lord
    all living cells
    Alleluia

PSALM 150
TRS. ERNESTO CARDENAL (B. 1915)

Heaven in Ordinarie

Prayer, the Churches banquet, Angels age,
God's breath in man returning to his birth,
The soul in paraphrase, heart in pilgrimage,
The Christian plummet sounding heav'n and earth;
Engine against th'Almightie, sinners towre,
Reversed thunder, Christ-side-piercing spear,
The six-daies world transposing in an houre,
A kind of tune, which all things heare and fear;
Softnesse, and peace, and joy, and love, and blisse,
Exalted Manna, gladnesse of the best,
Heaven in ordinarie, man well drest,
The milkie way, the bird of Paradise,
Church-bells beyond the starres heard, the souls bloud,
The land of spices; something understood.

GEORGE HERBERT (1593-1633)

The Soul at Home

Prayer is not a stratagem for occasional use,
a refuge to resort to now and then.
It is rather like an established residence
for the innermost self.
All things have a home: the bird has a nest,
the fox has a hole, the bee has a hive.
A soul without prayer is a soul without a home.
Weary, sobbing, the soul, after running through a world
festered with aimlessness, falsehoods and absurdities,
seeks a moment in which to gather up its scattered life,
in which to divest itself
of enforced pretensions and camouflage,
in which to simplify complexities,
in which to call for help without being a coward.
Such a home is prayer.

ABRAHAM JOSHUA HESCHEL (1902-1972)

A Living Word

Prayer is speaking God's name,
or rather, seeking God's name.
'What is your name?' – the eternal question
that comes back again after every answer.
It is the question asked by Moses
who met God as a 'difficult friend'
and talked with him 'as a man talks with his friend.'
Praying is trying to turn that little word 'God'
into a name that means something to me, to us, now.
It is trying to make that hazardous,
volatile little word really expressive.
You get nowhere if you say just 'God'.
Those three letters – they are just a code,
an unknown quantity, a stopgap.
You have to make the long journey from 'God',
a meaningless, boring, empty cliché,
to 'our God', 'my God', 'God of the living',
a meaningful, personal name
full of echoes of his entire history with mankind,
if you really want to pray.

> God, this word we call you by
> is almost dead and meaningless,
> transient and empty,
> like all the words we use.
> We ask you
> to renew its force and meaning,
> to make it once again
> a name that brings your promise to us.
> Make it a living word
> which tells us
> that you will be for us
> as you have always been –
> trustworthy and hidden
> and very close to us,
> our God, now and for ever.

HUUB OOSTERHUIS

God's Presence

God, I thank you for this time of prayer,
when I become conscious of your presence,
and lay before you my desires,
my hopes and my gratitude.
This consciousness, this inner certainty
of your presence, is my greatest blessing.
My life would be empty if I did not have it,
if I lost you in the maze of the world,
and if I did not return to you from time to time,
to be at one with you,
certain of your existence and your love.
It is good that you are with me
in all my difficulties and troubles,
and that I have in you a friend whose help is sure
and whose love never changes.

A JEWISH PRAYER

Attentive to God

Christians on both sides in this war
are claiming that I'm on their side,
and praying for me to prove it to the other side.

What am I supposed to do?
What am I even able to do?
Having given over my world
into the charge of human beings,
do they imagine I'm going to interfere from time to time
to show them they're not in charge at all?
Do those who pray hope to change my mind?
How preposterous! And how blasphemous.

I invented prayer not to make people more vocal,
but to make them more attentive.
I want them to pray,
not only for health and safety and peace,
but for the very air they breathe
and the bread they eat.
All is my gift.
I want them to realise that
they're not even strictly praying *to* me;
the very act of praying is my presence.
and my presence is not somewhere outside of them,
but in them and through them.

I don't act instead of them, but with them and in them.
If they want peace,
they must build it,
in the strength and wisdom I've given them.

God's Diary
H. J. RICHARDS (B. 1921)

Praise

Praise to the living God!
All praises to his name,
who was, and is, and is to be,
always the same;
the one eternal God,
before all else appears:
the First, the Last, beyond all thought
his timeless years.

Formless, all lovely forms
declare his loveliness;
holy, no holiness on earth
can his express;
for he is Lord of all,
creation speaks his praise,
and everywhere, above, below,
his will obeys.

His spirit surges free
and leads us where it will;
in prophet's word he spoke of old,
he answers still;
established is his law,
and changeless it shall stand,
engraved upon the human heart
in every land.

God gives eternal life
to every human soul;
his love shall be our strength and stay
while ages roll.
Praise to the living God!
All praises to his name,
who was, and is, and is to be,
always the same.

A JEWISH DOXOLOGY
TRS. JOHN BAILEY

8 BIDDING PRAYERS

I pray to you O Lord
from all my heart.
O Lord! I pray to you
with fervour and zeal,
for the sufferings of the humiliated;
for the uncertainty of those who wait;
for the non-return of the dead;
for the helplessness of the dying;
for the sadness of the misunderstood;
for those who request in vain;
for all those abused, scorned and disdained;
for the silly, the wicked, the miserable;
for those who hurry in pain to the nearest physician;
for those who return from work
    with trembling and anguished hearts to their homes;
for those who are roughly treated and pushed aside;
for those who are hissed on the stage;
for those who are clumsy, ugly, tiresome and dull;
for the weak, the beaten, the oppressed;
for those who cannot find rest during long sleepless nights;
for those who are afraid of death;
for those who wait in pharmacies;
for those who have missed the train;
for all the inhabitants of our earth
    and all their pains and troubles,
    their worries, sufferings, disappointments,
    all their griefs, afflictions, sorrows,
    longings, failures, defeats;
for everything which is not joy,
    comfort, happiness, bliss . . .
Let these shine for ever upon them
    with tender love and brightness,
I pray to you O Lord most fervently –
I pray to you O Lord from the depths of my heart.

JULJAN TUWIM (1894-1953)

9 A Selection of Collects

1 We remember, God,
how Jesus spoke about this world,
about you and about everything
to do with human life.
Something of what he said,
his words, his voice,
has been handed down to us –
enough to give us an idea
of who you are.
We pray that we may speak
the simple and understandable language
that he used.
We pray for all whose work it is
to preach the gospel
and to lead people in prayer.
May they never force you on people
or wrongly use your name.
We pray too for ourselves:
may we never run away from your silence,
but represent you as you are,
God so far and yet so near.

2   We thank you, Lord God almighty,
    for you are a God of human beings,
    and are not ashamed to be called our God,
    and you know us all by name,
    and you hold the world in your hands.
    And that is why you have created us
    and for this purpose called us into life
    that we should all be made one with you
    to be your people here on earth.
    Blessed are you, creator of all that is,
    blessed are you
    for giving us a place of freedom and of life,
    blessed are you
    for the light of our eyes
    and for the air we breathe.
    We thank you for the whole of creation,
    for all the works of your hands,
    and for all that you have done among us
    through Jesus Christ, our Lord.

3   God, it is your happiness and life
    that one son of man,
    of all the men born into this world,
    should go on living with us,
    and that one name should inspire us
    from generation to generation – Jesus Christ.
    We are gathered here in your presence
    to pray that we may hear and see him and pass on his name
    to all who wish to receive it.
    Let your Spirit move us
    to receive him from each other,
    and from you,
    this man who is our future,
    who lives with you
    for all people, for the whole world.

4   Lord God,
     you were happy to give us
     the light of our eyes
     and to let us be born.
     You did not make us
     for darkness and death,
     but so that we should,
     with all our hearts,
     live and come closer to you.
     Be merciful to us, then,
     and take us by the hand,
     and lead us to life
     today and for ever.

5   Lord God,
     you have given your Son to us.
     He was a man and, like us, mortal.
     He can understand and help us
     because he too has suffered
     and been put to the test.
     We pray that we too
     may mature in adversity,
     and be able to help
     and understand each other,
     and that we may,
     in all temptation and sinfulness,
     always hold on to him,
     today and all the days
     of our lives.

6   How many times, God,
have we been told
that you are no stranger,
remote from those who call upon you
in prayer!
O let us see, God,
and know in our lives now
that those words are true.
Give us faith
and give us the joy
of recognizing your Son,
Jesus Christ,
our saviour, in our midst.

7   Do not turn from us, God,
and do not avoid us
now that we are looking
for words to pray to you.
For if we call you God
and speak your name,
we do so because you have promised
that you will not be far
from all who call upon you.

8   Not for death, Lord, but to live –
that is why you made us.
Send us your Spirit,
give us the power
to become people,
whatever it may cost us.
May we not chase after emptiness,
run away from the truth,
forget your name.
May we hasten the coming
of your kingdom
and accomplish your will,
share the bread of this world
with each other
and be quick to forgive
all the harm that is done to us.

9   Lord God,
you have called us
from far and near.
You have made us –
great and small,
each one of us different
in heart and face,
but all of us your people.
We ask you, then,
make new people of us
who hear your voice
with living hearts.
Do this today
and never take your hands
away from us.

10   Lord our God,
great, eternal, wonderful,
utterly to be trusted:
you give life to us all,
you help those who come to you,
you give hope to those who call on you.
Forgive our sins, secret and open,
and rid us of every habit of thought
that is foreign to the gospel.
Set our hearts and consciences at peace,
so that we may bring our prayers to you
confidently and without fear,
through Jesus Christ, our Lord.

11   Lord, we are often afraid.
What do you mean by telling us not to be afraid?
Although no doubt it is true from your end
that nothing in life or death
can separate us from your love,
it mostly does not feel true from our end.
Even the very edge of the shadow of death
is enough to make us feel cut off from light and air.
Save us, Lord, we beg you.
May the rescue which you have made true in Christ
be true in our own experience too.
for his love's sake.

12   Father, our hearts are glad
because of the birth, and childhood, and manhood of Jesus.
We thank you that in every phase and aspect of his life
we are enabled to see yourself.
He is your embodiment:
the light of his character is the light of your glory.
May the inspiration of our worship come from him.
May the Church fulfil its calling to be his embodiment.
In each Christian may Christ be incarnate by faith,
so that his light may shine before people through us all,
and his glory become the ground of praise to you
from the whole world, for ever and ever.

13   *God of Abraham*, we praise you,
because early in history you called Abraham,
and so won his confidence that he left home for your sake
and struck out into the desert
not knowing where he was to go.
We praise you for his faith
and the truth about you that he learned
through his obedience.

God of Abraham and God of Jesus Christ, we praise you
because at the centre of history
you revealed yourself as never before.
We praise you for Jesus's confidence in you,
so great that he trusted you to the end,
and we thank you for the final truth about your love
which dawned on mankind through him.

God of Abraham, God of Jesus Christ and our God,
we praise you because you still come to us,
calling us to leave our present security
for an unknown future,
and promising that you will be with us
wherever we go.
You are with us now.
Help us so to worship that we trust you more fully
as we go further along the road of faith.

14   Lord, I have no idea where I am going.
I do not see the road ahead of me.
I cannot know for certain where it will end.
Nor do I really know myself,
and the fact that I think I am following your will
does not mean that I am actually doing so.
But I believe that the desire to please you
does in fact please you,
and I hope I have that desire in all that I am doing.
I hope that I will never do anything
apart from that desire.
And I know that if I do this
you will lead me by the right road,
though I may know nothing about it.
Therefore I will trust you always
though I may seem to be lost and in the shadow of death.
I will not fear, for you are ever with me,
and you will never leave me to face my perils alone.

15   Almighty God,
who has given us grace at this time
with one accord to make our common supplications to you:
and promised that when two or three
are gathered together in your name
you will grant their requests:
fulfil now, O Lord, the desires and petitions of your servants,
as may be most expedient for them;
granting us in this world knowledge of your truth,
and in the world to come life everlasting.

Index of Authors and Translators

ACKNOWLEDGEMENTS

Except where mentioned, the scripture readings in this anthology are translations by H. J. Richards, © 1995 by Kevin Mayhew Ltd.

The publishers wish to express their gratitude to the following for permission to reproduce copyright material in this publication:

Burns & Oates Ltd, Wellwood, North Farm Road, Tunbridge Wells, Kent TN2 3DR for *Lord, I have no idea where I am going,* from 'Thoughts in Solitude' by Thomas Merton. Also for the extracts from 'Psalms of Struggle & Liberation' trs. by Ernesto Cardenal.

Columba Press, 93 The Rise, Mount Merrion, Blackrock, Co Dublin, Eire for *More Present Than Ever* and *Attentive to God,* taken from 'God's Diary' by H. J. Richards.

Peter De Rosa for *Come, Holy Spirit, Spirit of Peace* and *Light of the World.*

Dimension Books Inc., PO Box 811, Denville, New Jersey 07834, USA for *The Kiss of God,* from 'The Face of God' by Archbishop Joseph Raya © 1974.

The Ecologist, Agriculture House, Bath Road, Sturminster Newton, Dorset DT10 1DU for *The God I Need* by Andrew Darlington, from 'The Ecologist' November 1974.

Editions du Seuil, 27 rue Jacob, 75261 Paris, France for *A World Transformed* by Petru Dumitriu, from 'Incognito', Collins 1964.

Epworth Press, Hartley Victoria College, Luther King House, Brighton Grove, Manchester M14 5JP for *Despair is Indecent,* from 'The Hammer of the Lord' by Colin Morris.

Faber and Faber Ltd, 3 Queen Square, London WC1N 3AU for *A Great Cry,* from 'Report to Greco' by Nikos Kazantzakis.

HarperCollins Publishers, 77-85 Fulham Palace Road, Hammersmith, London W6 8JB for *Spirit of Jesus,* from 'On Being a Christian' by Hans Küng.

Anne Lewis for *I believe in God,* taken from the 'Epworth Review' January 1991. This creed forms the centre of an unpublished collection of poems 'Dreams and Rhythms of Love' reflecting on ministry in the inner city.

McCrimmon Publishing Co Ltd, 10-12 High Street, Great Wakering, Southend-on-Sea, Essex SS3 0EQ for *Christians believe,* from 'The Creed for Children' trs. H. J. Richards. Also for *A Proper Man* by Estelle White, from 'You Can't Climb a River'.

Rev Dr Colin Morris for *Why God Hides Himself* from 'Christ and the Cosmos' published by Westminster College, Oxford, OX2 9AT.

Mowbrays, an imprint of Cassell Plc, Wellington House, 125 Strand, London WC2R 0BB for *God's Love Let Loose,* from 'Consider Jesus' by Elizabeth A Johnson, Mowbray 1990. Also for *Sharing Christ's Spirit* by H. J. Richards, from 'The Miracles of Jesus', Mowbray 1983.

Continued overleaf

Stewart; *I believe in the living God* by
Huub Oosterhuis; *This is the Man* by
James Brabazon; *Why He Came* by
Fr René Fumoleau; *Trustfulness* by
Ignaz Maybaum; *Only Seeds* (anon.);
Our Man (anon); *Our Lord the Man* by
Père A. Duval and *Hope for Everyone*
by Samuel Halkin.